AS WHEN WAKING

PHOENIX POETS
Edited by Srikanth Reddy
Rosa Alcalá, Douglas Kearney &
Katie Peterson, consulting editors

As When Waking

DANIEL SCHONNING

THE UNIVERSITY OF CHICAGO PRESS
CHICAGO & LONDON

The University of Chicago Press, Chicago 60637
The University of Chicago Press, Ltd., London
©2025 by The University of Chicago
All rights reserved. No part of this book may be used or reproduced in any manner whatsoever without written permission, except in the case of brief quotations in critical articles and reviews. For more information, contact the University of Chicago Press, 1427 E. 60th St., Chicago, IL 60637.
Published 2025
Printed in the United States of America

34 33 32 31 30 29 28 27 26 25   1 2 3 4 5

ISBN-13: 978-0-226-84384-1 (paper)
ISBN-13: 978-0-226-84385-8 (ebook)
DOI: https://doi.org/10.7208/chicago/9780226843858.001.0001

Library of Congress Cataloging-in-Publication Data

Names: Schonning, Daniel, author.
Title: As when waking / Daniel Schonning.
Other titles: Phoenix poets.
Description: Chicago ; London : The University of Chicago Press, 2025. | Series: Phoenix poets | Includes bibliographical references.
Identifiers: LCCN 2025015457 | ISBN 9780226843841 (paperback) | ISBN 9780226843858 (ebook)
Subjects: LCGFT: Poetry. | Abecedariuses.
Classification: LCC PS3619.C45376 A93 2025 | DDC 811/.6—dc23/eng/20250408
LC record available at https://lccn.loc.gov/2025015457

♾ This paper meets the requirements of ANSI/NISO Z39.48-1992 (Permanence of Paper).

Authorized Representative for EU General Product Safety Regulation (GPSR) queries: **Easy Access System Europe**—Mustamäe tee 50, 10621 Tallinn, Estonia, gpsr.requests@easproject.com
Any other queries: https://press.uchicago.edu/press/contact.html

For Geoff Babbitt

> *I know, I feel*
> *the meaning that words hide;*
> *they are anagrams, cryptograms,*
> *little boxes, conditioned*
> *to hatch butterflies . . .*

H. D., *The Walls Do Not Fall*

CONTENTS

Proem 3
Paean 11
One Poem About Poetry 12
Catalog 13
[Little Box: Caedmon and the Host] 15
Midwinter Elegy 16
Body Moving About a Frame 17
[Little Box: Honeybee] 18
Dog Star 19
The Beatitudes 20
[Little Box: Gilgamesh and Enkidu] 22
As When Waking 23
Ladder 24
A Perfect Form Unblinking 26
[Little Box: The Vulture and the Jackal] 28
The Living 29
A Vision 30
[Little Box: Juniper] 31
The Machine (I & II) 32
Scales 37
[Little Box: Coyote and the Quail] 39
Birdsong 40
Coda 41
Origin Story 42
[Little Box: Ezekiel and the Word] 43

The Material World 44
Catalog 46
Copper War Statues 48
[Little Box: Sundiata and Sogolon] 50
Catalog 51
Hagiographies 53
[Little Box: Purple Martins] 55
Four Koans 56
Prayer Is Better Than Sleep 58
[Little Box: Sappho and Orpheus] 60
Alphabet 61
Postlude 62

Acknowledgments 71
Notes on the Text 77

AS WHEN WAKING

Proem

At first, it's as if all things are

At first, it's as if all
things are words

At first, it's as if all
words are raining
and from their forms, forms fall

At first, it's as if all things
are one word

At first, there is nothing

but the terrible lightning

And when the storm subsides, the catchbasin
coos; the sky exhales; the dead rosebush withers;
the bright kingfisher paces in the sand.

And all night, the lemon tree remembers
sun. And the bathhouse cradles the salt spring,
casts its bodies in white steam. And the earth

opens for the spade. And the moon jar sings
from its dark womb, holds its breath. And the crow
turns and turns in the blue air. And the sickle brings

the meadow back to earth; the meadow
mourns its shadow. And the aspen shakes
green, red, gold. And all morning, the ghosts

low from the crooks of oaks; the nightjar wakes
to listen. And the father brings his children
to the shore. And the aging clockmaker

thinks, as she must, about entropy. And
the kindling crackles in the marble hearth.
And the octopus sleeps like a stone, changes

color while he dreams. And the lone train car
splits the fog across its nose. And the belfry
shutters its windows, hides its brass heart.

And in the east's deep ocean, sand lifts—briefly—
as if to carry on to somewhere
new; there, in pools of shadow, so do the

drowned ones lift—too briefly—as if to bear
north, retake the beachhead, wander wildly
into some fresh havoc or wonder or

neighbor at the fair. And the xiphoid spines
of prickly pears erupt in pods of seven.
And the green blackberries dot the green vines.

And the orb weavers have built an open
curtain through which the yellow porch light spills.
And the icicle falls from the eave like an

apricot. And the coyotes keep their kills
in earthen dens, catch snowflakes in the cold.
And the shoots of blue grama, of purple

aster, of little bluestem, shiver so
softly in the west's bare wind. And the moon's
dull humming makes ripples in the pond.

And the white marble busts of the dead bloom
from their dark hall. And the willow leaves
brush against barbed-wire fences. And the loon

dives into the lake. And the deep well sees
Lyra, even at midday. And the warbler
parts the lemon of its rind. And the marquee

keeps its eyes in a bronze bin. And the north's
soft heather cranes to see the morning sun.
And the cube of sugar forgets its form

for the warm black tea. And the mother runs
upon the metal bridge. And when light
returns to the valley, the kestrel drums

along the bough; the red cedars blush white;
the mu'adhdhin sings, his voice like a drawn bow.
And the cherry blossoms cut through the night.

And the fishing trawler, arms akimbo,
teeters to shore like an infant. And the cliff
swallows have built their nests of mud below

the chimney's tin crown. And the south's cold mist
pours down the rain-wet hill. And the water
bear purrs. And the child leans into the wind,

makes his body large. And the lighthouse keeper
can't help but imagine. And the skies
above the mountain's peak are brighter

than the snow. And the temple roof curls wide
to catch the summer rain. And the glassblower
turns the white-hot sphere. And the wet clay shakes alive.

And, yes, the wild zinnias open their eyes.

Paean
After H. D.'s "Heat"

Apple
blossoms
curl their
delicate
ends: make
fists in air. April, the minor
god, spills his wet breath on the orchard—
hurls his
ice and wind. After days above, the yellow-
jacket must return to its clay den. The bright
kernel of sun still
lifts along its old path,
muted—made a soft and perfect circle by the clouds' white veil. O
nectar light,
O
plenum, O
quiescent star—
rend the pale
sky by its seams.
Turn the cold
under; turn it other. Pour yourself, again, into the
vellum-colored earth; make it
wet with light. Let this
xylem drink of
you; let each blossom be its own
zygotic sun.

One Poem About Poetry

By noon, an old man on a unicycle is navigating the seven-part ramp at Spring
Creek Overpass. He moves haltingly
downward, pausing at
each landing to turn.
For every time I think he might stumble,
grab the handrail, fall over one side,
he only shudders
in place—forward, back, forward—
juddering on by degrees. The
kinetics are hardly efficient (one could more easily
lug the thing down the adjacent set of stairs), but if this
man wanted efficiency, he would
not be riding a unicycle.
On the fourth plane, his
pace
quickens—he
rolls on and back with abandon. Across the
street, I try to hide my gaze, pretend
that he, his yellow helmet, and his sky-blue
unicycle are as daily as anything. Still, I hope that he might notice me there,
voyeuristic. I hope that, if he were to look up, his sunglasses
would slip to the bridge of his nose—he would gaze through the
X-patterned grate, and we would lock eyes. We would laugh together,
yelp for the joy of it. But he doesn't look. Instead, he proceeds with his private
zeal to the road, then
away—eyes inscrutable in their bliss.

Catalog

Crescent moor. at
dawn.

Egg-white canvas, empty but for ribs of
feathers. Clay pot on its side.

Groan of wooden beams. Hand- and foot-
holds, flat and firm.

Iris, prairie fire.
Jasmine, fleabane, phlox. Beetle-

kill pines.
Landfill.

Mountain crag, full as a
nesting doll.

Ova. A person-like
personal god. Three

quick strokes of
red.

Stone
thrushes

underfoot. Green
vale. Ground cinnamon.

Winter. Little
x's in sand.

Yellow dusk-gibbous. White neck of jacket
zipper.

Altar. Ivory
button with three eyes.

[Little Box: Caedmon and the Host]

(The cowherd dreams of angels.

All day, his heavy head
has felt like a box of
quivering butterflies—

He sleeps on a bare cot
stuffed with juniper leaves
beside three dozing calves—

When the cowherd wakes, he sings.)

Midwinter Elegy

"Do lilies return?" Yes,
every spring. Most do—most do in
flocks. "But you know what I mean. Do they
grow again? Their same bodies? I
had forgotten the word *perennial*.
I've forgotten so many things—the sound
jackrabbits make when they're
killed, though I remember the hush of their bowed
legs bounding through the snow. Why
most,
not all?" Some are
only called lilies, are really annuals—
planted and tended, only to die that year. Others struggle—others drown
quiet in their beds. "And the
rest? You know what I mean: Are they
still
the same? Each spring,
under their
violet feathers, do new
water-flecked
xeranthemums bloom? Is my
yellow
zephyr's song—lace folds and
all—its own? When winter pulls
back its white mantle, reopens the earth, who
comes back to me?"

Body Moving About a Frame

Exercise One: Building your
four-sided box.

Guide Level: Beginner.

Historical Origin: Beishouling, located
in modern-day Baoji, China,
just fifty miles (eighty
kilometers) from the Three Kingdoms period's
longest and oldest wooden bridge (unusable).

Materials: Cabinet-grade maple (¾" × 4'× 8'), table saw,
nail gun, spool of paperbound finishing nails (galvanized),
oil finish (or oil and varnish mix), wood glue,
pewter handles (×4), titanium hinges (×2),
quilted fabric (~ten yd., cotton crepe,
royal blue and white lattice), down stuffing, needle, thread (depicted in Fig. 1).

Starting Out: Before assembly, measure and cut maple boards
to desired height and width
(understanding possible
volumetric change—likely increase in
weight, likely decrease in height
[x inches per year, depending on
yearly rainfall, humidity
zone, diet, and proximity to the equator]—
and possible change in aesthetic or religious
beliefs in interval before use).

Combining Parts:
Depicted in Fig. 2.

[Little Box: Honeybee]

While I watch from the hall,
a lone dazed honeybee
stings the oak-top table—

(Late June; nearly the equinox.

The sun is falling to the east.)

The bee flies, leaves behind
one long thread of herself
like a compass pointing—

Dog Star

From the gnarled
garden hedge, a
havoc of damselflies bursts.

In the paintbrush shadows of late spring morning,
juniper shrubs
knit the wet air.

Light cradles the leaves' dark lattice. Light
marks the
naked form, holds
open its
parts. Light moves
quiet as nothing.

Real things ask
so little of us.

The damselflies settle
under the old redbud tree, awash in its
violet shadow.

Wind arranges the soft
X of their wings. Wind curls the grasses'
yellow ends, rattles the low
zenobia like so many bells. Wind moves
always away.

Behind the sky's stark-blue shell,
Canis Major walks into the waiting
dark. Real things ask nothing—not

even to be seen.

The Beatitudes

God says to the meek one, "On Sunday mornings, have them say 'Yes'—
    say 'Yes,' brightly.
Have them nestle dollar bills in the knots of elm trees; use three times
    the zest in their lemon curds.
If it's snowing, open the flue and start up the fire. Tell them there's a
    double Dutch
jump rope with their name on it. Paint the windows violet; paint the
    lattice pink. Tell them every
knock-kneed great blue heron is just like me: long legs, quick eyes, and
    chock-full of
longing. Tell them I've got a real doozy of a crossword clue that I just
    can't get—eight letters, ends with an *x*." So the

meek one says, "All right"—goes to the window, sets his yellow work
    gloves on the sill. He could
not be more tired. His fingers have that tingling feeling, like they're
    boiling—it must be below zero outside, he thinks, too cold for walking.
    But it's plenty warm in here. If he's honest, the meek one's had
one hell of a day. His mother's dying—can only eat bananas, milk,
    and bits of uncooked dough. He can't
put it out of his mind. Her voice is thinning out a little more each
    morning: When she wakes up crying, it sounds like a kestrel singing
    from far off. Sounds like she's got a
question stuck in her throat. What that means to the meek one, he doesn't
    know. For now, he's waiting for the snow to fall a little softer, for the
room to darken, so he can keep *x*-ing the boxes on his to-do list. At least
    it's warm here, he thinks. God says to the meek one, "On

Sunday evenings, have them bundle their children in blankets made of
    pansies—yellow over blue—then hunker down for the night. And if
    they have to leave, remind them
to zip up their coats—it's ice-cold out there. In the crawl space

under that double-wide, there's a nest of jaybirds—tell them not to look
    or the birds are sure to
vanish. Ask if, sometimes, everyone would just keep quiet.
When a foghorn lows at night, pours itself out on the salt reeds and
    beaches, rattles the pier's
X-shaped pilons, and sets the gulls flying, ask if they'll just listen." So the
    meek one says, "All right"—keeps looking through the window.
    There's a grove of

young aspen trees—"daughters," they're called—laid bare by the cold.
    The meek one is not sure they'll make it. A gray snowbird
zips from one naked branch to the next and the meek one thinks
about his mother. She'll be getting hungry soon. She mostly stays in bed,
    but yesterday the meek one found her crumpled on the
bathroom floor. Her long hair—always in a neat high bun—was spread
    wide on the slate, bright as zinc. One summer, when the roads were
    dirt and the roof was tin, a thunderhead
crawled through town like a freight train—no rain, no hail, just hot wind
    and lightning. At the time, the meek one's mother said the storm could
    take the house right off its feet; would
draw the meek one clear up to heaven if he didn't just stay put in that
    bathroom, hold tight to the hot water valve, and hope—said she'd be
    right back. But the meek one couldn't help it. When the storm shook
    the house, he ran to the main room and peered out the window.

Even in the half-light, the meek one saw his mother at once. She was lying
    on the knoll outside, holding quick to two fistfuls of grass—watching the
    black cloud fill and empty with long threads of light. She was speaking
    into the wind. The warm air surged against her upturned face, drew
    skyward a havoc of her black hair. At the time, the meek one thought
    she might have been saying "Please."
From the other room, the meek one hears his mother wake and try to rise.
    The light dims. He slips his gloves into his back pocket, takes up his list,
    and marks one box with an *x*. Turning from the window, the meek one
    says, "All right."

[Little Box: Gilgamesh and Enkidu]

(Gilgamesh knows a dozen secret things.

He knows that his friend, quiet
Enkidu, is just clay
and water; that he loves him—

He knows that, next, he must ask
his friend to fight sleepless
Humbaba in his lair—

He knows Humbaba sees but cannot dream.)

As When Waking
For Maura Callahan

Heads tucked
into the dark
jamb of breast and wing, the mallards sleep in
knots. Two dozen of them
litter the blue ice—doze against waves frozen
mid-curl. Bright cracks fissure the pond like
neurons, like veins, like
oak branches advancing into the open air—
presence kin to absence—
quiet
ruptures, all. While the mallards
suck winter sun into
their dark backs, they dream their way into the pond's green
underneath—
vie
with half-open eyes for the muddy floor. Light filters down in
X's, runs its fingers through the gloom. When dreaming, as when waking,
    the mallards can do little else but
yearn: for a pure-white sun stalled at its
zenith; for round-edged bits of
apple
bread; for yet more
cold and knotted bodies with whom to share the
day. Above all, they dream that—somewhere under all this ice, where they
    can one day find it—there is an
egg-shaped hole in the
floor of the world, from which all
good things swim.

Ladder

"Infant" comes from the Latin word for "speechless," which is to say
June bugs and heather and white-orange
koi fish are—in their silence—childlike. But
language is replete with these sorts of
misgivings. "Net," despite its form, shares no root with "nest."

❦

"Nerve" arrives from "nervus," which refers both to the marionette-like
    tug of tendons in
one's arm and the taut strings on a lyre. How does the word—spoken, sung—
pull its listener? The infant ear?

❦

"Quintessential" comes from the Latin *quinta essentia*, meaning "fifth essence."
    In the Old World of elements and alchemists, whatever was
residual was believed fundamental, transcendent—the stuff of
souls. Language is residual of this thinking, which is to say language
transcends it. "Cloud" comes from the Old English *clüd*, meaning "rock."

❦

Under a winter anvil head, snow filters down in streaks of blue-gray, a motion called
"virga," wherein the solid form sublimes—turns
water, then vapor, then turns away—without ever touching the earth. This
    movement finds a natural counterpart in
"xylem," the tendon-like
yellow of a plant, which allows liquid to climb across its parts—
    "transcend" them. So survives the wild
zinnia, the mountain heather, and the midwinter
apple grove.

"Believe" comes from the Proto-Indo-European "to love," and rightly so.
    I love the water that
climbs its great ladder of air; I love the
dark nets sunk in dark seas to
encircle the gleaming bodies therein; I love the body's
filaments, its nerves, its
gossamer strings that run our lengths again and again; I love the song
    made by nests of quaking
heather just before the storm.

A Perfect Form Unblinking
Unto the Whole—how add?—Emily Dickinson

Just down the autumn beach, a hive of honeybees teems—its mouth
    the open door to a yellow-hot
kiln. The world, it seems, is overfull. Wet ocean air
leaves beads on saw grass clusters

marking the inland sand like shadow. Somewhere out of sight, the moon is
    lurking dark and
new. The clouds above blush a sun-hungry purple. The low
ocean extends its long tongue—

pale rose
quartz—
rakes and rakes its

soft white
teeth
upon the sand.

Violet light washes down in eddies,
washing the world gray. But the honeybees—

Xanthos-like, manes
yolk-bright—
zip and

alight on the
bluestar's
collar;

draw out its color. It seems
every given thing is nuzzling the next, is
full to brimming, is a perfect form unblinking. Past the hive, a corpse-tree points

godward, its Socratic arm
heavy at the joint. Bluestar, honeybee, honeybee:
I have lost all sense for walls. One thing is full of the other.
    I'm pointing, too.

[Little Box: The Vulture and the Jackal]

(The vulture tells the mourners to depart;
    their child has died.

The heart can't maneuver this
maze of grief; if it could, the heart
would rather quit, stand still, and starve—

But the mind exceeds so many
small horrors; all their ugly forms
are, in time, made dark and lovely—

The jackal tells the mourners to return;
    their child will live.)

The Living
After Kathryn Cowles's "*Clouds. Eleanor Eleanor.* Acrylic on Canvas. 2005"

Kid with Satellite. Daniel Schonning. Palette wood, thread,
lemon rind, aluminum foil over papier-
mâché. *Painting of a
Newborn Looking Deeply
on the Texture of Red Leaves* or
*Potter's Child in
Quilt of Leaves*. Daniel Schonning. Oil on pine board. *Absent Father
Reimagined as Three-Eyed Angel*. Daniel
Schonning. Egg shells (chicken,
tern, pintail duck), powdered aspirin,
used matches, mechanical pencil on linoleum counter.
*Violence and Its
Wet Edges* or *God of War, God of Love*. Daniel Schonning.
Xylograph on
yew board. *Fall Harvest in Childhood*. Daniel Schonning.
Zinc intaglio with nitric
acid, lemon juice,
bitumen,
candle wax. *Self-Portrait as Sudden Summer
Downpour at
Evening (as Viewed Through a Single-Paned Skylight, Inches
from the Artist's Nose)*. Daniel Schonning.
Gouache on paper.
How to Mourn the Living. Daniel Schonning. Empty carton of
    Carlton cigarettes, nine forty-watt
incandescent bulbs (clear glass), car battery, lemon seed, half-empty handle of
Jack Daniel's whiskey, ball-peen hammer.

A Vision

Listen: What I say next I
mean precisely. Yesterday, at
noon, while I was weeding the war memorial just south of Edora Park,
    a door
opened in the earth. This is no metaphor. I mean,
precisely, that a silver doorknob sprouted from nothing, that its
    appearance set the bindweed
quaking. I mean that, where the gleaming sphere
rose, long seams unspooled in the granite
slabs—formed the transom,
the threshold, etched a word in its center. I had spent the morning there
under an open August sky, just outside the ponderosas' round shadows,
    pulling
vines of field bindweed from the ground. The plant produces
white flowers in the shape of trumpets—small enough to fit on a child's
    thumb—a dozen for every
X-hatched thicket. Each flower is milk white, soft
yellow at its center. Though much smaller, bindweed is sometimes known
    as "false morning glory," which calls to mind the night sky's
zodiacal light—what the poets have named "false dawn"—
and that strange celestial spearhead even resembles the bindweed's nascent
buds. What I mean is that, yesterday at noon, I was
culling the field of these gentle and prostrate things, tearing their
delicate forms from the dry
earth, when a doorknob sprouted
from nothing, when the black
granite—parting from itself quietly as clouds from
horizon—formed the transom, the threshold, one word
in its breast. I mean that the bindweed shook its many heads, that a cluster of
jaybirds went spinning madly from the pines, and that as I
knelt beside the silver orb—my hands still wrapped in vines—
    I could not move to turn it.

[Little Box: Juniper]

When I was eleven,
they felled the juniper
that grazed our small blue house—

(In every poem is a quiet thing that it means
    to keep safe.

If this poem had an icebox, its quiet thing
    would be inside.)

At ten, in its branches,
I found a honeycomb
full of yellow nectar—

The Machine (I & II)

I

Maenads tore Orpheus to pieces. On
Nysa Mountain, at dawn, Orpheus prayed
on the temple steps, bathed in the new sun,

plucked in praise the white lyre Hermes made.
Quilts of starlings rose from the dark forest,
rippled across their lengths. The poet sang,

So the world opens. So it must, it must—
The Muses stirred in their distant sleep, dreamed
unseeing of the brute blood, the torn breast,

viscera on the temple steps. The mean
waters of River Hebrus—like listing
Xanthos—flowed warm and cold as he sang, teemed

yellow, as if with hair of a low god listening.
Zephyr lilies leaned close; green yews shook; the blind
aphids ceased, for a moment, their slow killing.

Behind Orpheus, where they knew his mind
could not dwell, the maenads neared; poured from their
dark quarters like Python out of Delphi;

eluded—in their frenzy—the bright air
folding aegis-like around the poet's form. They
gored him where he stood. The light faltered. A bare

horror followed—one in which quiet lay
in the mouths of all things like an obol.
Just as the raving ones pulled his head away,

knelt and thrust it in the Hebrus, the bold
lyre sounded—drawn by wind. The poet sang.

II

Never, O gods, has a sky been so open—

Orpheus drifted on the subtle waves,
purled down Nysa Mountain like a
question. At his passing, the siltstone blazed

red; the cattails foamed white; bright clouds of
silver midgeflies sieved the morning mist.
The poet sang, *Never, O gods—a body so*

unraveled—

       —Long before Orpheus—before his lyre rode on currents of
          wind, before his
voice echoed through the valley's bright
womb—Nysa Mountain stood above all else. Its great temple cut the
   horizon in two—

      —Long before Orpheus, the head of Nysa Mountain
              broke from its shoulders—

xiphoid shards of black granite burst
      from its peak—

     —Long before Orpheus, stones scattered across the valley, shepherds
       puzzled them into walls all along
         the pale-green hills—

    —Long before Orpheus, in the valleys' low meadows,
     among riots of white
yarrow, great boulders settled against one another

    like clutches of eggs;

  farmers circled their plows about the strange forms
      so that the field's long furrows

     appeared as ripples
     from where the rocks fell—

  —Long before Orpheus, spear-shaped fragments struck
   the earth and stood upright;

zealots prayed at the feet of the dark spires that,

   long before Orpheus,
   were once Nysa Mountain—

And above Orpheus, Apollo's white lyre played on air, each note soft
 and strange as
breathing. And the poet sang: *O gods, O gods, I am at last a navel—a pure
circle, budding*—And his itinerant head, like the bright temple far above, was

drawn taut along the edge of bare
earth, wild river, and open sky.
Finally, the poet—like Zeus, whose mother

> *O gods, O gods, I am at last a navel—*
> *O gods, O gods, I am a small glass circle—*
> *An open eye, a mouth, O gods, O gods, O gods—*

guarded the infant god from his father's eye,
handed Kronos the omphalos to be swallowed
instead—found himself singing in the bright

> *Never, O gods, a body with no center—*
> *Never, O gods, a center simple and bare—*
> *The sky, O gods, O gods, O gods—*

jade voice of river stones. He sang of his own
katabasis, when Tantalus last drank. He sang
low and long of his own longing—*O gods, I am at last a*

> *O gods, O gods, I am at last a machine*
> *O gods, O gods, I am at last a machine*
> *made of wanting—empty but for everything—*

machine made of wanting—empty but for everything—

Scales

Once, when he was a boy, Paul's father took him into the city
    to visit the big bank.
Paul had never been to the city. He was the youngest of his
    four siblings and the
quietest—he mostly listened and looked, looked and thought.
    To get to the bank, Paul and his father
rode the blue bus, which made
stops in two other towns along the way. At the first, a
tall woman boarded with a stuffed dog tucked
under her arm. She sat two rows ahead of Paul and his father
    with the gray bundle facing behind her so that, when Paul
    pressed his face into the gap between the black
vinyl seats, he saw the dog's two glass eyes looking back at him.
    Paul looked so long that,
when at last he blinked and leaned back beside his father, he felt little
X's on his cheeks from where the seat covers wrinkled. Paul ran
    his fingers along the marks and thought of the
yellowing hand mirror his mother used to keep beside the bed—
    zig here, he touched his face;
zag there, he touched the seat. When the bus entered the city
at last, Paul looked up and saw that every seat was filled,
but he didn't know how—he couldn't remember stopping in the
    second town at all. There was a lot that Paul didn't know,
couldn't remember. His mother used to say that Paul was so deep
    in his own head, she wished he would grow a little window,
    just so she could see him way
down there. Walking into town some days, Paul would turn around and
    realize that his family had kept going when he stopped to look on a
    tangle of wild poppies, or a colony of
earwigs, or the unattended basket of eggs at the end of the Marcuses'
    long dirt drive—*Take what you need, leave what you can*, the sign
    said, and Paul couldn't

figure why his father never took any, never even stopped. But some things,
    Paul thought, are
good not knowing—Paul knew lots of things he wished he didn't—only it's
hard to tell before you know them. When Paul and his father disembarked,
    it was nearly dark. The bank would have to wait until tomorrow. Paul's
    father took his hand
in his, tighter than normal, and hurried them along toward the stuffy motel.
    As they left the bus station, Paul forgot to see where the tall woman with
    the gray dog was headed, like he'd planned to—instead, he
just looked through the station's clear plastic roof at the bright metal
    buildings that loomed high above them and at the hard edge of his
    father's jaw. And even though he saw his father crying that night in
    the motel, and again on the ride home the next afternoon, Paul was
    glad they came—he learned all
kinds of things in the city. For one, not all windows open. Another:
    Even in that strange place, where the sky held more
lit-up hallways and kitchens and bedrooms than stars, if Paul craned
    his neck down the right alley, he could still see the half-
moon way up there. Last: At night in the city, when looking from far off,
    an unlit window—especially one that does
not open—can sometimes look so dark, it's easy to imagine someone
    behind the glass, looking back.

[Little Box: Coyote and the Quail]

(Coyote wants to see the whole horizon.

All summer, his eyes have
felt like two hungry mouths,
like two jaws fixed open—

He throws his eyes atop
the desert willow, where
its pink blossoms gather light—

Coyote sees, far off, two quail nodding home.)

Birdsong

"Place cannot be body," writes Aristotle,
"qua containing, it is different from the matter." He's
restating one of Zeno's paradoxes. Put
simply: The cicada's shell is not
the insect, even while it's worn. But what you and I
understand, reader, is that place makes a body. The
vesper iris is named not only for
when it blooms but also for where—along the marble
xyst of a far-off monastery, its blue lips
yawn open (for a moment) to receive the evening prayer. Are its dark
    inner folds place? Its green stalk?
Zeno would say no. In his vision of place, nothing grows; a child
    walking home never
arrives; arrows stall and dissolve mid-flight—their ghosts thickening
    the summer air like
birdsong. But, reader, we know the world to be otherwise. See how the
    Kentucky warbler's brittle
clutch of new-laid eggs curls opposite the nest's round palm. Who first
drew together the debris of a space—bound the
even-threaded twigs and pale strips of bark, the dry
ferns, and still-green
grasses—into a world-made womb? Who chose the first naked crook of
hawthorn or honeysuckle on which to create?

I must stop to tell you, reader, as I've only
just learned: If a cowbird lays its eggs in that same nest, a
Kentucky warbler will simply build another over top.
Left underneath, the eggs—warbler and cowbird both—
might yet hatch, might tremble and call out. But they have already
    ceased to be bodies.
Now, in their dark net of tree and reed, they are part
of place—are only womb through which the next clutch comes.

Coda
After Dan Beachy-Quick

Quiet is a body
riddled with song.

So goes the hymnal so goes
the parish: Prayers are useless
unless sung. Quiet is an illusion
vibrating in place. Elusive particle
wave wave wave wave
xylophonic ribs in indefinite sky.

Yellow meadowlark, the hill's
zealous bell. Quiet's push and pull.

All the hymnals
blown to hell. Particle
collision. Hollow knell.

During fission and solar
eclipses, all the birds
fall quiet when all
goes dark. There is no
heaven where there
is no song. No heavens.

Jupiter's moon is a small blue
knot. It has no birds, it is not
living but leaves living
marks on the dark.

No hymn. Jupiter's moon knows
only its one water-song:
perfect quiet in three parts.

Origin Story

Really: The wind is purling through the glade, just so, as if to mutter
something darkly in
the mouth of a jar. Really:

Unless the river means it, there won't be
violets; there won't be
willows, so there won't be aspirin or fishing nets made from strips of willow
xylem some ten thousand
years ago; there won't be elegant or common
zinnias; there won't be mountain field mint; there won't be
apricot saplings, unless the river means it. Really:

Blue-bellied clouds
carry the river overhead. Really:

During the hurricane, I was a teen; I was caught out alone; I had to
edge through my hometown one
flooded road at a time. I would stop the car,
get out, test the moving water, and go on. I looked for a branch and found a tree.
Hidden in the canopy was a spool of yarn, somehow pinned,
its yellow nest uncurling. Really:

June is when matter of all
kinds and colors bludgeons the air. Really:

Lifting from the dark
meadow, whole
nebulae
of cornflowers are
pregnant with rain. All at once they
quiver, speak.

[Little Box: Ezekiel and the Word]

(Ezekiel can hear God creeping in the far bushes.

High above him, the dusk
light untangles itself
from the wet southern wind—

Far behind him, the broad
jade-faced mountains cradle
yellow meadows of flax—

When Ezekiel approaches, the bushes go quiet.)

The Material World

Shadows of birds are sweeping again across my closed eyes and I am
    breathless
trying to name them. For weeks I've thought nearly without pause about
    what's
under this river of light and lack and I think that the effort might carry
    me with it. I can see in silhouette the
V-shaped crooks of these creatures' limbs and count the rough-edged
    feathers in each tail such that this one might be called
"waterloom" for the splay of its long talons and that one "silverfish" as
    its two anterior quills cross to form a tender
X so very like antennae. These days I think often on Catherine Blake
    (who signed her wedding contract to William with only an *X*) to
    whom so many of her husband's works owe their
yellows blues and reds. Her task was to carry sunlight and its scatterings
    onto what was left by the bare copper or
zinc or otherwise flood with watercolor the white valleys of his reliefs.
    Heraclitus pictured
an afterlife wherein our wet souls perceive by smelling (wet because
    moisture conveys scent all the
better) and I believe this to be the truth. It stands to reason then that
Catherine was the only one to know the chemical souls of those prints
    and that when the works one day
die (as they must) it ought to be in rain. This is all to say that the
    light and lack afflicting my closed
eyes are at times so dense as to be nearly liquid which is to say I can
    nearly smell it. Now a dozen shadows
flit past at once and I am tempted to call them all "blackberry cluster"
    though I'm certain I've used the name already on a
group that passed yesterday. They were so many and carried on for so
    long that I began to lose my
hold on which was matter and which its absence. William once asked
    "Then tell me, what is the Material World, and

is it dead?" and I find myself wondering the same. If I had to express the
    almost-scent of this light it might be something like
juniper leaves in August cupped by flush-red palms. That it is the only
    thing I smell tells me that I haven't yet died or at least that I'm the
    only soul in my
ken and that these shadows are something else altogether. Every now
    and again there passes one
long-winged seabird that I've named "Los" and the last time it visited
    I thought I could distantly sense its eyes
moving to follow me as it circled. Still I could
not smell it. These days I think so often
on what Catherine made of her works before she gave them color.
    I wonder whether she found the
prints and metal plates (rendered simply in folds of white and black) at
    all heartbreaking. I believe she did. Three more shadows swell and
quietly recede. I name the first "satyr." I name the thin one that melds
    with the light "pale
red foal." I name the last "raincloud" as it hovers overhead (for what
    feels like an eternity) before dissolving.

Catalog

Telephone wire
under bright winter raincloud.

Vulture. Host of
waterbugs.

Xeric shrubs in
yellow desert.

Za'atar in glass bowl. Dried
apricots.

Billowing
curtain over open

door.
Empty canvas but for strings of right-

facing parentheses.
Gallery.

Hands in jacket pockets. Chickenwire sculpture, shaking
in bed of rust-spotted

Jeep. Cold
kiln. Unsigned

letter. Midsummer
moonlight, water-thick. Complex of white pine

needles
on cemetery

path. Larkspur buds.
Quilted winter

raincloud under bright
sun.

Copper War Statues

Unless a belief is nearly-too-hot to hold, I think it isn't sincere.
    For example, there was a battered red
VW Beetle for sale when I finished my first summer cleaning classrooms,
    moving bookshelves, and
waxing floors at the old middle school in town, and I remember drawing an
x on the ad for it like they do in movies—the asking price was exactly
    what had been
yielded by my summer's work, and someone that age takes those sorts of
    things as meaningful, regardless of gas, insurance, etc., etc.—after all,
    before that summer I had
zilch in the way of money, the family house was just foreclosed on and we
    didn't see a cent from it, we were moved into low-income housing, and
    right then, I was holding by a thread to

a faith that I didn't understand, which is to say I believed in God in
    the eyes-half-shut way that the Soviets must have when reading
    one afternoon that—despite no
bombs being dropped or lines of defense being breached or rebellions being
    waged—their whole
country was really just an idea and the one person thinking hard until that
    second to make it so had
died all of a sudden, and so everything was going to have to change, might
    have changed already—and I can imagine that a few of the people who
    were told this new truth chose not to believe it,
even preferred to imagine that they could, all of a sudden, be the ones
    thinking so hard as to give back
form to the places and ideals of their childhoods, could pretend as if they
    hadn't picked up the paper that day or
given a ride to that stranger who mentioned in passing the sudden change in
    the morning light, the
hands of children holding their books just so, and the strange sense in the
    city center that

it all had crumbled and been rebuilt overnight so that the stone walkway and the
    cinema marquee and the copper war statues were replaced to look
just as they were yesterday, before everyone slept, but that this time they
    were all made purposefully *without* something, though it was hard to
know what that something might be.

        I believed in God in precisely this way and therefore

let that conviction seep into my every insight of the world, including the
    uninterrogated feeling that
my first car was to be a red VW Beetle from the early '80s that looked to
    need three times the asking price just to run, though even
now I can still remember the near-giddy sense of joy I took in its faults,
    especially the dent
over the front driver's side wheel well and the general matte finish that,
    even when
pictured in the glossy advertisement, clearly expressed a brittleness—
    even weariness. But the
quiet look it had about it was determined and said something like,
    "Yes, it ought not to make sense, but
red red red, if you can believe it—red dent, red morning, red marquee.
    A simple world full of red
simple things, each of which is simply where it ought to be."
The car I bought was blue.

[Little Box: Sundiata and Sogolon]

(The djali said the boy would one day grow mightier
    than Alexander.

When he was born, Sundiata was so
quiet that his mother feared him dead;
he gazed up at her, silent and still—

On the seventh day of her child's life,
Sogolon bent and whispered the boy's
two names in his right ear, a prayer—

After seven years, the hero walked; he hunted
    with an iron bow.)

Catalog

Venus beside
waxing half-moon.

Xenolith on striped gneiss. White
yarrow, blue oak.

Zinc coins in
applewood box. Fits of

beard lichen along low
cedar boughs. Morning mist.

Damselfly nymph. Fast-
eroding coast,

fast-
growing

hills. Low humming. Angel
in green glass jug. Red

jump rope draped over white sill.
Kerosene

lamp. Cotton wick.
Midsummer shed with

no roof—full
of glass milk bottles—

perfectly
quiet before

rain. Granite.
Strike-anywhere match.

Telephone. Mars above
upturned crescent moon.

Hagiographies
    After Robert Hass's "What the Modernists
    Wrote About: An Informal Survey"

When he was thirty-one, Wittgenstein worked at a small grammar school
    in the Austrian hills, helping students solve for
x. Having already served in the Great War and written what would be the
    first of his major works, the still-
young philosopher gave up his family fortune and settled in the rural steam
    town of Trattenbach, hoping that he could quiet "all the devils" loose
    inside him. Once there, he found the local guesthouse,
"Zum braunen Hirschen," too full of music and so elected to sleep on a cot
    in the school's kitchen.
According to the headmaster, Wittgenstein would spend his nights sitting
    at the small window, watching the stars.

🦋

Baraka grew up in Newark, New Jersey, in an "orange house with a porch
    you sit on, or
crawl under and plot shit." He played baseball
down the street from his home, in the vacant lot facing the Newark Street
    Jail, where
eventually he would get locked up during the Newark Rebellion—where
    he would see
(from his cell window) the National
Guard murder a couple in their car—their car parked in
his same vacant lot. Back then, his name was LeRoi Jones. Later, he changed
    it to Blessing.

🦋

If the reader could look out from one of Niedecker's poems and into the
    place where they were written, they would see her one-room cottage.
    In it:

jumbles of books and papers, a wood-burning stove, a table, a bed, and a
    wet red rug stretched between two chairs to dry. Nothing else. The
    poet spent most of her life there, alone on Blackhawk Island—"a finger
    pointing into Lake
Koshkonong, Wisconsin"—which flooded so often that there was no clear
    year-round boundary between water and
land. Her "Paean to Place" begins, "And the place / was water." From her
    one room, the poet
made do. One sunny afternoon, after days and days alone with the rain,
    the muddy water receded at last and
Niedecker settled at her desk to write.
"O my floating life / Do not save love / for things / Throw *things* /
    to the flood."

🦋

Paradise could be an old farmhouse with fruit trees—so believed Bronson
    Alcott. So he said to everyone from Massachusetts to Ohio, though most
questioned the idea. The transcendentalist and his thirteen followers
    thought that if they disavowed all the
rest of it—ate very little, wore thin white linens (though never wool and
    never cotton),
sang of the seed and the fruit—they could reenter the Garden, could find
    it right there at an old farmhouse with fruit
trees. After Alcott's experiment failed—when his followers quit and he ran
    out of money and the place was left to crumble—that notion of living
    never left the man. He kept believing
until the idea took hold in his friend Thoreau. The latter's paradise was a
    small wooden house on a site that "some might have thought too far
    from the
village." Thoreau lived two years, two months, and two days in "an airy
    and unplastered cabin, fit to entertain a travelling god."

[Little Box: Purple Martins]

The purple martins sleep in
a box made for peaches
with nine small boxes therein—

(Mid-July, the daylight moves in quilts.

The sky is closer than it was.)

From the middlemost square,
in a nest of hazel leaves,
the smallest martin sings—

Four Koans

X asks Z, "Where do
you find the word?"
Z replies,
"Are the reedlings silent
before they alight on the rostrum?"

🕊

"Can a body move outside the ten
directions?" a monk asks Master
E. Master E answers, "A person
falling doesn't
give thought to where they thrust their
hand. A person dreaming moves only
in."

🕊

J is pruning a young
kōyamaki pine in the temple courtyard. An apprentice
leans from a high window and asks,
"Master, the pine
needles beyond the temple are shed
only by the wind and the rain—who are you to
prune them?" J looks
quizzically at his pupil and
replies, "So be it." He pulls the
sapling from its bed and
throws it over the temple wall.

Upon entering the monastery, Master M pauses in thought. She points to its vaulted ceiling and says,
"When the heavens draw near as your own roof, you will know the word."

Prayer Is Better Than Sleep
For Nina T. McKee

Years ago, I was leaving my front door on Ahmad
Zaki Street in Amman when I saw
a woman with long white hair—she seemed to
be pregnant—
crossing the street again and again, her head
down, looking for something.

Earlier that morning, I woke to the *adhān al-fajr*—found a piece of paper
folded three times on itself and pinned to the inside of my bedroom door.
    I must have
gotten up in the middle of the night and
hung it there (the door was still locked), but I couldn't remember waking.
Inside, written in letters
just like mine, the paper said, *We enter and exit. We write our poems alone.*

🕊

Kneeling on the edge of the
lake—that lake too large to see the other side—a tall
man is crying into his hands.

🕊

Near the mouth of Bristol Channel,
on the Welsh side, there's a castle called St. Donat's. A dear friend and I
    were living there, training to helm the A-shaped boats used to save
people lost at sea (though *lost* is the wrong word—too
quiet, too faultless). I barely slept that summer and so remember those
    days as I remember dreams.

Rolling each afternoon in the brackish waters, our
small boats cut the sea into patterns—"the grid," "the gyre,"
"the quincunx"—while we searched the waves for imagined human forms.
    Always we worked
under the steady gaze of St. Donat's high black battlements, in the company
    of slate-gray carrier
vessels (which, despite the surf, were as still as gravestones) waiting at
    anchor for a port of entry to beckon them in.

When our time in Wales was nearly over, we took the boats far out to sea.
    The water was all whitecaps, and the sky a mess of colors. As we bobbed
    in place, a long white
X appeared on the far horizon, approached, then passed perfectly overhead.

[Little Box: Sappho and Orpheus]

(The poet wakes to distant music.

All night, she might have dreamed
singing on the sea air;
a quiet voice, pleading—

She descends the black cliffs,
finds a half-drowned onyx bust
jutting from the azure waves—

When she lifts the stone, the poet sings.)

Alphabet

Zinnias and apple blossoms appear and appear and appear
across the sun-bright orchard, and the honey-
bees are swimming from them, back to honey-
colored hives, cradling their
delicate song—

Each geometric
fold in the apiary is a
golden letter singing and the great
hive is an alphabet, a song
in which each letter appears
just once—

Knowing (as the hive does) that the
letter (like the honeybee) is
matter and memory, is wax and
nectar, is a half-
open window and a wet
plaster mold—knowing
(quiet as they are) that the dark-
red honey is the only
song that the honeybee can sing,
that the bright apple blossom is an
Ur-sound stranger than song, that (up close) the white stamens rattle like
vertebrae in the warm April
wind—knowing it all, the honeybee alights on the apple tree's
X-shaped petals, faces at last the
yellow sun—

Postlude

At last, it's as if all things are

At last, it's as if all
things are letters

At last, it's as if all
letters are waves, and from within
they pull, they pull

At last, one poem washes up
on the shore of another

At last, there is nothing

but moonlight and wind

And where the dry clay crumbles, the forest
path unspools; the red sun flickers; the mound
ants fold into the earth. And the gosling

drags its breast through dark threads of grass. And the
storm simpers, turns its insides out—spins south
at last, to die. And all night, the great ash

doors of row houses are closed, each one perfect as
any other. And the white trellis is nearly
gone under a havoc of cucumber

leaves. And the notes are letters; the letters are
too many to count. And the bright poplar tree
means to fade to sky. And the museum's long

rooms pretend against time; there, the daughter
pulls her mother by the hand. And the
wound pours itself empty. And the coyote says,

You'll never see me again; the high window
asks, *Where does it all go?*; the defunct
shuttle loom hums, *These things need time*. And at

last, the north's great millstone turns itself to
nothing. And the boy has found a worn
brass key, which, on every door, he can't help

trying. And the boat's metal mast rattles the
quarter-moon. And the chimney smoke is still
lifting, lifting—gone. And the pointed heads of

sugar beets part the soft brown earth. And the
lapwing wanders here and there. And the light seeps
under the door. And the sky casts its yellow

wind. And the tops of nails protrude, their O-
shaped mouths agape like medieval angels
singing. And the heifers settle in pools of

shade, with faces sweet and sad. And the old men
cross their legs at the knee. And the west's high stream
cradles the mountain field. And in the graveyard,

moss and lichen vanish the dead; the black
xysts whiten; stone faces bunch under the crypt's cornice—
watch the rain. And across the east's pale

forest, the bowerbird gathers bits of
song. And the plow exhumes the ancient pot,
gives back its air to air. And far off,

among amber clouds, Mercury is small as
sand. And at twilight, green Venus circles
alone, like a blind fish in its limestone cave.

And the moon surveys the earth from its round
crook in the great red cedar. And Mars spins on its minor
slant, lifts the light like yarn. And Jupiter's

arc is straight and clean as the cantilevered
flight of magpies. And Saturn holds Titan
hard—kneads, kneads, kneads its center warm. And

like the cat's eye, Sirius fades from blue
to green. And in the dawn-sick cluster of Pleiades
light cleaves one body to the other. And all morning

blue filters from the sun like water drawn
from snow. And high on the autumn hill, the
yellow sign says *Yield*. And the distant minaret

hums. And, all day, the riverfish curls quiet
in the willow's black roots. And the wasp makes a room
of the stone-hard fig. And the live oak reaches farther

still, rests its elbows on the earth. And the butter
dish clinks into place. And the field mouse finds
something sweet in everything it tastes. And the red

bricks quiver; the stonemason tires and stills. And the
hand can still remember the small dead things
it's held. And the thread points back to center.

And the voices cease. And the loose earth settles.
And the asphodels draw their shadows close.
And the bellows fill once more with breath.

And the wild zinnias, yes, close their eyes.

ACKNOWLEDGMENTS

Grateful acknowledgment to the editors of the following publications for first featuring versions of these works:

The Carolina Quarterly: "Alphabet," "Birdsong," and "Origin Story"
Crazyhorse (now *swamp pink*): "Proem" (as "Aleph with all, all with Aleph")
The Hopkins Review: "Dog Star" (as "Pneuma")
Orion Magazine: "[Little Box: Juniper]" (as "[When I was eleven]")
Poetry Daily: "Birdsong"
Poetry Magazine: "The Beatitudes" (as "Abecedarian 'G'")
Puerto del Sol: "Paean" and "A Perfect Form Unblinking" (as "Plenum")
Washington Square Review: "Body Moving About a Frame" (as "Bodies Moving About a Frame")
West Branch: "Catalog" ("Telephone wire . . .") and "Ladder"
The Yale Review: "As When Waking"

    My thanks to Srikanth Reddy for his extraordinary care and generous eye in selecting and editing this book. To be a part of the Phoenix Poets series is the honor of a lifetime. Immense thanks, too, to Rosa Alcalá, Douglas Kearney, and Katie Peterson for thinking the manuscript worthy of publication and for their careful attention and time. Thanks to David Olsen, McKenna Smith, and the whole team at the University of Chicago Press for their stewardship of this book and for making it into the beautiful object that it is.

🦋

To Dan Beachy-Quick, without whom this book would never have existed; whose ethic, insight, and generosity ushered every one of the above poems into the world.

To Kathryn Cowles, for her stalwart mentorship, friendship, and mind-opening poetics; for being the very first and very best person to show me what it means to be an artist.

To Camille T. Dungy, whose ears and eyes radically shaped the poems in this collection and who offered an entirely new way to pay attention.

To Harrison Candelaria Fletcher, who showed me what it means to be a teacher, a reader, and an *essai*-ist.

To Stephanie G'Schwind, who taught me how to tend both to the written word and to one's community of writers—and, perhaps just as vitally, taught me the correct spelling of *all right*.

🦋

To Susannah Lodge-Rigal, without whom I would come untethered; for dumpling soup, half-marathons, and long drives reading poems aloud.

To Kristin Macintyre, who is the person and poet I most aspire to be like; for indie movies, mountain treks, and beachside napping.

To Robin Walter (and Banjo and Fiddle), without whom I would scarcely have written a word worth reading; for bareback horse rides, family dinners, and the occasional criminal trespassing.

... To be in community with you three is one of the great gifts of my life.

🦋

To Noah Baldino (and Fanny), for, among so much love and editorial attention, their meditations on the immense difference between *the* and *this*.

To Eric Barnes (and Elfie), for trusting me with the hardest and loveliest job I've ever had; for his fierce advocacy, guidance, and friendship.

To Bethany Bradley, for breakfasts and books and backwoods cemetery excursions.

To Margaret Browne (and Peter), for ForkSocket prep and horror movies.

To Rob Carson (and Archie), whose priorities as an educator, scholar, and person have radically shaped my own.

To Esther Hayes (and Juniper and Turnip), without whom I wouldn't survive one minute of application season; for themed birthday parties, our weekly pool night, and handmade cards and stamps.

To Katherine Indermaur, for foothill hikes and poetic vision.

To Tara Furey, for bookstore gossip and vegan treats.

To Nina McKee, for Jordan and Greece and Wales; for sleepless ferry/plane/bus rides and '80s workout wear.

To Stacey Philbrick-Yadav, for offering whole new modes of making meaning; for showing me my place in the world.

To Jacob Powell, for a friendship steadier, gentler, and more generous than I thought possible.

To Ana Tresnan (and Albi and Hobart and Penny), for chaotic cross-country moves, dresses made of words, and lemonade ice tea; for more than a decade in community.

To Kira Witkin (and Kiwi), for a retreat from the world.

🐾

To Amira Abdulqadir, Kazim Ali, Kristy Beachy-Quick, Joe Braun, Cameron Breck, Casey Breen, Hannah Bright, Eleanor Brooks, Megan Clark, Calder Cowles, Remi Cowles, Sobin Cowles, Katy Craig, Annmarie Delfino, Hannah Dighton, Leila Einhorn, Christina Houseworth, Katherine Indermaur, Ingrid Keenan, Julie Liebenguth, Jack Martin, Alick McCallum, David Mucklow, Taylor Murray, Cherie Nelson, Timothy O'Keefe, Jordan Osborne, Steven Penner, Max Piersol, Vivienne Piersol, Matt Poiesz, Donald Revell, Kylan Rice, Evan Senie, Christa Shively, Natalia St. Lawrence, Mickey Stein, Aliceanna Stopher, Emily Surprenant, Stefan Tangen, Michelle Thomas, Tyler Toy, Jess Turner, Marie Turner, Kelly Weber, and C. L. Young.

🐾

To Peter Schonning, who remains the best reader and editor I know and whose influence affects my every word.

To Rory Schonning, whose first steps I followed so closely that I clipped their heels and whose example I try to follow still.

To Ann Callahan, for reading every draft of every poem she's ever been sent; for setting aside all the good stuff while volunteering at the library book sale; for, despite working two jobs to raise three kids alone, not balking at the prospect of one of them studying poetry; for each year better and better than the last.

To the whole Callahan clan—Bobby, Mickey, Patsy, Danny, Jeannie, Neily, Ann, and Tommy—and their partners, kids, and kids' kids. Thanks, especially, to Maura, Jeannie, and Shayne, each of whom is a pillar that holds me upright.

To the Depews—Honoré, Brittany, Émile, Ambrose, and Ursula—for game nights, dinners, soccer games, whiffleball tournaments, and basement dance parties; for being my home.

To Keagan Willemsen, Anzhela Antanova Willemsen, and Marat Antanov, for sometimes letting me win at bocce.

To the Schonnings and Feders—Gunnar Schonning Sr., Gail Feder, John Feder, David Feder, and Amy Feder.

To my colleagues and friends at Hobart and William Smith Colleges—Alex Black, Melanie Conroy-Goldman, Stephen Cope, Anna Creadick, Kevin Dunn, Laurence Erussard, Keoka Grayson, Amy Green, Alla Ivanchikova, Ingrid Keenan, David Kendrick, James McCorkle, Margaret Milella, Nicola Minott-Ahl, Ben Ristow, Mel Sage, Tina Smaldone, Angel Szymanek, and Anastasia Wilson.

To my teachers—Chris Abani, Andrew Altschul, Matthew Cooperman, Todd Mitchell, Mary Ruefle, Barbara Sebek, and Sasha Steensen.

To Coach Phil Lazzaro, whose example and influence has given me the parts of my life I cherish most and whose belief in me has made everything else possible.

To Diane Mahoney, whose attention, care, and encouragement solidified writing as the center of my life's gravity.

To Aitor Lajarin Encina, for the influence of his brilliant art and yet more brilliant friendship.

To Del Harrow, for including me in his beautiful series and entrusting me with his space.

To Jane C. Huffman, for her generous reflection on "Paean" and poetic influence in *The Hopkins Review*.

To my students—Bella Babikian, Malique Bailey, Cyma Berk, Leo Bonacci, Neve Cawley, Hudson Chou, Maggie Farwell, Rachel Faust, Seamus Galvin, Jasmine Goncalves, Luis Gontes, Awa Haidara, Sreyan Kanungo, William Koepp, Hussein Labib, Gianluca LoPorto, Ksusha Lowry-Neufeld, Michelle Mangione, Kyle Mast,

Diya Moolani, Elim Pilet, Kayla Powers, Lamia Nur Rahman, Annabel Ramsay, Tay Rossi, Jacob Siegel, Fairooj Suhita, Sandeep Tissaaratchy, Kate Villinski, Natalie Whitehair, July Winters, and Mohammad Yassin.

 And, lastly, all my gratitude to Geoff Babbitt, to whom this book is dedicated—for passing the fire.

NOTES ON THE TEXT

The book's epigraph is an excerpt of *Trilogy* by Hilda Doolittle, copyright © 1945 by Oxford University Press; Copyright renewed 1973 by Norman Holmes Pearson. Reprinted by permission of New Directions Publishing Corp. and Carcanet Press Ltd.

The title for "One Poem About Poetry" alludes to George Oppen's "Five Poems About Poetry," in *New Collected Poems* (New Directions, 2008).

The opening gesture of "Midwinter Elegy" is borrowed, with gratitude, from Julie Liebenguth's conversation with the author.

The tone and invocation of "A Vision" is owed to the title piece of Brigit Pegeen Kelly's "Song," in *Song* (BOA Editions, 1994).

The word "godward" in "A Perfect Form Unblinking" is borrowed, with gratitude, from Kristin Macintyre's "Lush the Cradle," an unpublished manuscript shared with the author.

The formal and sonic work of "Coda" is inspired by Dan Beachy-Quick's "Draw Near," an unpublished manuscript shared with the author.

The quoted sections of "Hagiographies" are derived from Ray Monk's *Ludwig Wittgenstein: The Duty of Genius* (Penguin, 1991), Amiri Baraka's *The Autobiography of LeRoi Jones* (Freundlich Books, 1984), Jonathan Ellis' *Letter Writing Among Poets* (Edinburgh University Press, 2015), Lorine Niedecker's "Paean to Place," in *Collected Works* (University of California, 2002), and Henry David Thoreau's *Walden; or, Life in the Woods* (Ticknor and Fields, 1854).

In "Postlude," the "blind fish in its limestone cave" is borrowed from Yusef Komunyakaa's *Night Animals* (Sarabande Books, 2020).

A Note on Form

In writing this book, I've tried to apprentice myself to the essential work of letters—to listen to and learn from the systems and symmetries found therein. The alphabet serves as this book's catalyst and container, its medium and constraint.

Twenty-six of the poems are abecedarians, in which the initial letters of each line advance in alphabetical order, with the first poem moving from *a* through *z*, the next from *b* through *a*, and so on. Some of the poems adhere to (or eschew) additional forms therein.

"The Beatitudes" follows an invented form I've named the "lattice abecedarian," which revisits all the letters of the alphabet in a fixed sequence once per stanza. "The Machine (I & II)" works through the abecedarian form on its left margin and terza rima on its right, until that pressure causes the piece to break, scatter, and re-form.

The first and final poems of the book also progress via terza rima on their right and left margins, respectively, through twenty-two iterations of rhyme. This kind of formalism owes a debt to the *Sefer Yetzirah*, which explores—through a Jewish mystical framework—the relationship between the twenty-two letters of the Hebrew alphabet and the world that they inhabit.

The recurring "Little Box" poems follow another invented form I've named after the image in the book's epigraph from H. D. Each of these poems is a syllabic pangram, a minimalist container in which each letter of the alphabet appears at least once.